Prince Harry
Mar

The biography

Introduction

Prince Henry of Wales, also known as Prince Harry, is the second son of Charles, Prince of Wales, and Princess Diana. After enduring the death of his mother in 1997, he occasionally acted out and found himself in the tabloids for embarrassing events. Prince Harry embarked on a decade-long stint in the military in 2005, seeing active service time in Afghanistan, and is involved in numerous charitable causes.

Meghan Markle pursued a career as a screen actress, appearing in a number of TV series before landing the role of Rachel Zane on the USA Network show Suits. Markle, who also ran the lifestyle blog The Tig from 2014 to 2017, became the subject of international headlines in 2016 upon the revelation of her romance with Prince Harry of Great Britain.

After announcing their engagement in late 2017, the two married on May 19, 2018, and welcomed son Archie Harrison Mountbatten-Windsor the following May. In January 2020, the couple revealed plans to step back from their senior roles in the royal family.

This is the descriptive, concise biography of Prince Harry & Meghan Markle.

Table of Contents

Enjoy all our books for free...

  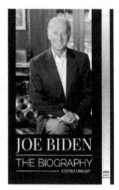

Interesting biographies, engaging introductions, and more.

Join the exclusive United Library reviewers club!

You will get a new book delivered in your inbox every Friday.

Join us today, go to: https://campsite.bio/unitedlibrary

Part 1: Prince Harry, Duke of Sussex

Prince **Henry, Duke of Sussex,** born *Henry Charles Albert David* on 15 September 1984 at St Mary's Hospital, Paddington, London, is a member of the British Royal Family. Grandson of Queen Elizabeth II and Prince Philip, Duke of Edinburgh, he is the second son of Charles, Prince of Wales and Lady Diana Spencer.

Harry is sixth in the order of succession to the British throne, behind his father Prince Charles, his older brother Prince William, Duke of Cambridge, and the latter's three children, George, Charlotte and Louis.

From 2010 to 2015, he was an Army Air Corps helicopter pilot after serving as an officer in the *Blues and Royals*, including participation in the war in Afghanistan in 2007.

On May 19, 2018, Harry marries American actress Meghan Markle and receives from the Queen the title of Duke of Sussex.

After March 31, 2020, the Duke and Duchess of Sussex were removed from the Royal Family to lead a financially independent existence. They relinquish their royal representative duties and all public remuneration, and no longer use their predicate of royal highnesses.

Biography

Youth and studies

From the age of four, Harry goes to Jane Mynors preschool a few days a week. Two years later, he joined his brother William at the prestigious Wetherby School in London before going to Ludgrove School in Berkshire.

In 1998, he was admitted to Eton College. There he studied geography, art and art history. In June 2003, he completed his studies at Eton with two A-Levels, obtaining a B in Art and a D in Geography. He dropped out of Art History after the AS level. He excels in sports, especially polo and rugby.

With his degree in hand, Harry took a year's sabbatical. He stays in Africa and Argentina. Then in Australia (like his father in his youth) in a breeding station. He takes part in a polo match between England and Australia. He also goes to Lesotho where he works with orphan children and produces the documentary film *The Forgotten Kingdom*.

Prince Harry devotes a large part of his free time to sports: polo, rugby, skiing and motocross.

Military Career

Training

In officer training at the Royal Military Academy of Sandhurst from May 2005 to April 2006, the Prince asked to join the British troops stationed in Helmand in Afghanistan fighting the Taliban. He even threatened, if refused, to leave the army, or even the United Kingdom, to go and live in Africa. He declared in 2005: "there is no question of me going through Sandhurst and then going home and letting my guys go and fight for their country.

Afghanistan War

In May 2007, Prince Harry was scheduled to join British troops in Iraq, but his commitment was cancelled because military authorities feared that insurgents would do everything possible to capture him. General Dannatt finally decides to send him to serve in Afghanistan, with the understanding that he may change his mind if circumstances change. He goes there under the false identity of "Harry Wales".

In February 2008, an American website reveals that Prince Harry is in Afghanistan. The British Ministry of Defence decided to evacuate him immediately and explained in a press release: "Following an accurate risk assessment by the chain of command, it was decided ... to remove Prince Harry from Afghanistan immediately. This decision was made primarily because global media coverage of Prince Harry's presence in Afghanistan could have an impact on the safety of all those deployed in that country, as well as pose risks to himself as a soldier. [...] Until Prince Harry returns to the UK, we ask the media to avoid speculation about his whereabouts, the timing of his return and the route he will take. Some media were already aware of the Prince's presence in Afghanistan, but preferred not to reveal it.

The princely military adventure will have lasted ten weeks. The *Daily Mirror* specifies: "He took part in patrols in the dangerous province of Helmand and he wiped out the enemy fire like any soldier". On March [1,] 2008, Prince Harry returned to the United Kingdom. (The Ministry of Defence announced on the same day that Prince William was also expected to serve during 2008 on a *Royal Navy* ship that could be deployed in the South Atlantic, the Persian Gulf and the Pacific.) For his service in Afghanistan, Prince Harry was decorated by his aunt, Anne, Princess Royal, with the Afghanistan Operational Service Medal at Combermere Barracks in West London on May 5, 2008.

Army Air Corps

In October 2008, information filtered through about Prince Harry's desire to fly military helicopters. After passing the initial aptitude test, Harry, who uses the alias "Harry Wales," completes a month-long evaluation as an Army flying personnel at Army Air Corps Base (AAC) Middle Wallop. The result is to determine if he can move on to Apache, Lynx or Gazelle helicopter pilot training.

Prince Harry received his "wings" (his pilot's license) from his father on May 7, 2010 during a ceremony at the Army Air Corps base in Middle Wallop. The Prince also announced that he intends to fly Apache attack helicopters if he successfully completes the rigorous Apache training course. After which he will be able to return to active service, again on the front line, in one of the war zones where the British Army is engaged. At the May 7 ceremony, he exchanged his black and red Blues & Royals cap for the Army Air Corps sky blue beret, adorned with his Household Division insignia.

On March 10, 2011, it is announced that Prince Harry has successfully completed his test flight on Apache. He receives his Apache Flying badge on April 14, 2011. He is promoted captain in April 2011 and expresses the wish to return to Afghanistan. He completes his Apache helicopter training with a twelve-week internship in the United States at the end of 2011. On July 8, 2013, Lieutenant-Colonel Tom de la Rue, his supervisor, announced that he had passed his Apache helicopter captain's exam.

Staff

In January 2014, Prince Harry joins the staff where he oversees the organization of various events such as the commemorations of the First World War or the Warriors Games.

Resignation from the army

On March 16, 2015, Prince Harry announced his resignation from the army, which he will leave in the summer of 2015. He justifies his decision by the fact that, as he can never again serve in the field (for security reasons linked to his royal status), an administrative career in the General Staff does not suit him. Prince Harry served the British Army for

10 years. On June 19, he left the army, in which he served as Harry Wales.

Military ranks

- May 8, 2005 - April 13, 2006 : Cadet Officer
- April 13, 2006 - April 13, 2008 : Cornet (Second Lieutenant) (Household Cavalry *Blues & Royals)*
- April 13, 2008 - April 16, 2011: Lieutenant (Household Cavalry *Blues & Royals)*
- since April 16, 2011 : Captain (Army Air Corps)
- since May 14, 2018: Squadron Leader (Royal Air Force)

In December 2017, he succeeded the Duke of Edinburgh as Captain General of the Royal Marines, a position he left on 31 March 2020.

Royal Functions

At the age of 21, Prince Harry was appointed Councillor of State. He began to carry out his royal duties abroad with his grandmother The Queen at the Commonwealth Heads of State and Government Conference in Malta in 2005. The following year in Lesotho, he again visited the Mants'as Children's Home near Mohale's Hoek and, with Prince Seeiso of Lesotho, launched Sentebale, the Princes' Fund for Lesotho, a charity for children orphaned by the human immunodeficiency virus/AIDS. It also gives its patronage to a number of other organizations, including WellChild, Dolen Cymru, and MapAction. With Sentebale's help, Harry and his brother organized the concert for Diana at Wembley Stadium on July [1] 2007. He has also been a sponsor of the English Rugby Football Union (RFU) since 2004.

Through sport, Harry helps charities and other organizations that train students as a development officer for the Rugby

Football Union. He also participates in polo games, like his brother and father, to raise funds for charities.

On January 6, 2009, Harry and his brother Prince William get their own royal house from their grandmother, Queen Elizabeth II. They operate with a small team led by Sir David Manning, former British Ambassador to Washington, as part-time advisor to the princes (previously, William and Harry's business was handled by the office at Clarence House in London). On this occasion, it was announced that they had established their own office at St. James' Palace to handle their public, military and charitable activities. New monograms then appeared on their correspondence. Harry has one, similar to his brother's, but with an H in a shades of blue, similar to that used by his mother.

In March 2011, the Prince returns to his charitable commitments, and lands in the heart of the Arctic, on the Svalbard archipelago, to undertake an expedition to the North Pole. The purpose of this initiative is to raise funds for the association Walking With The Wounded, which helps wounded soldiers (rehabilitation, reintegration into the world of work, etc.).

On his wedding day with Meghan Markle, May 19, 2018, Harry is created Duke of Sussex by his grandmother Queen Elizabeth II, with the subsidiary titles of Earl of Dumbarton (Scotland) and Baron Kilkeel (Northern Ireland).

Departure of the royal family

In January 2020, Prince Harry and his wife announced their intention to become financially independent by renouncing most of their public commitments and to live between North America and England, which was soon nicknamed "Megxit". They retain their title of Duke and Duchess of Sussex, but renounce their predicate of Royal Highnesses, that of Royal Highness (without being stripped of it) as well as all public remuneration, no longer being active in the Royal Family as of March 31, 2020.

They also lose the right to use the word "*royal*" and their police protection. In addition, the couple will have to pay rent for Frogmore Cottage, a mansion in Windsor Park that remains their British base, and reimburse the taxpayer for the £2.4 million ('2.8 million) spent on its renovation. However, Queen Elizabeth said she was always ready to welcome them if they changed their minds.

After a few months in Vancouver, Canada, they moved to Los Angeles, California, where Meghan's mother lives, and near Hollywood where Meghan plans to resume her career.

On 19 January 2020, after the final agreement, Prince Harry gave his "exit speech"

"Good evening, and thank you for being here for Sentebale, a charity me and Prince Seeiso created back in 2006 to honor my mother's legacy in supporting those effected by HIV and AIDS.

"Before I begin, I must say that I can only imagine what you may have heard or perhaps read over the last few weeks...

So, I want you to hear the truth from me, as much as I can share -- not as a Prince, or a Duke, but as Harry, the same person that many of you have watched grow up over the last 35 years -- but with a clearer perspective.

The UK is my home and a place that I love. That will never change.

I have grown up feeling support from so many of you, and I watched as you welcomed Meghan with open arms as you saw me find the love and happiness that I had hoped for all my life. Finally, the second son of Diana got hitched, hurray!

I also know you've come to know me well enough over all these years to trust that the woman I chose as my wife upholds the same values as I do. And she does, and she's the same woman I fell in love with.

We both do everything we can to fly the flag and carry out our roles for this country with pride. Once Meghan and I were married, we were excited, we were hopeful, and we were here to serve.

For those reasons, it brings me great sadness that it has come to this.

The decision that I have made for my wife and I to step back, is not one I made lightly. It was so many months of talks after so many years of challenges. And I know I haven't always gotten it right, but as far as this goes, there really was no other option.

What I want to make clear is we're not walking away, and we certainly aren't walking away from you. Our hope was to continue serving the Queen, the Commonwealth, and my military associations, but without public funding. Unfortunately, that wasn't possible.

I've accepted this, knowing that it doesn't change who I am or how committed I am. But I hope that helps you understand what it had to come to, that I would step my family back from all I have ever known, to take a step forward into what I hope can be a more peaceful life.

I was born into this life, and it is a great honor to serve my country and the Queen.

When I lost my mum 23 years ago, you took me under your wing.

You've looked out for me for so long, but the media is a powerful force, and my hope is one day our collective support for each other can be more powerful because this is so much bigger than just us.

It has been our privilege to serve you, and we will continue to lead a life of service.

It has also been a privilege to meet so many of you, and to feel your excitement for our son Archie, who saw snow for the first time the other day and thought it was bloody brilliant!

I will always have the utmost respect for my grandmother, my commander-in-chief, and I am incredibly grateful to her and the rest of my family, for the support they have shown Meghan and I over the last few months.

I will continue to be the same man who holds his country dear and dedicates his life to supporting the causes, charities and military communities that are so important to me.

Together, you have given me an education about living. And this role has taught me more about what is right and just than I could have ever imagined. We are taking a leap of faith - thank you for giving me the courage to take this next step.

So ... welcome to Richard's garden -- minus the fountain!

First, may I echo Johnny's words earlier and thank in particular Patricia and Richard, and all the teams involved in making tonight so very special and such a success... at least so far...

Thank you also for turning up!

I'm sure Lewis was the draw factor, but I know you will all be leaving tonight with a better understanding about what we're trying to achieve at Sentebale, and that's what really matters to us.

I first visited Lesotho many years ago, back in 2004, and was shown around by my dear friend Prince Seeiso -- who sadly isn't able to join us this evening.

Struck by the hardship and challenges so many children faced, and with the support of local partners, we set up Sentebale two years later. The word Sentebale means "forget me not" in Sesotho and also serves as a memory of both Prince Seeiso's mother as well as my own.

Since the beginning, we've developed a series of programs and created the purpose built Mamahato centre to help a generation of children break through the stigma that is allowing the HIV epidemic to thrive. Half of those children had lost either one or both of their parents to the virus.

But today through our networks of clubs, camps and programs across both Lesotho and Botswana, we help children and young adults to learn that they can go on to live happy and productive lives, despite being HIV positive.

We teach them that this human immunodeficiency virus doesn't have to be a death sentence for anyone anymore, that the real enemy we are fighting is stigma, and the antiquated attitudes that work against young people coming forward when wanting to take an HIV test.

This is relevant in every part of the world today, including here in the UK, where there are an estimated 110,000 people living with HIV.

Here, I can't not mention my dear friend Gareth Thomas -- who in my mind -- has quite literally changed the way people think about HIV -- so thank you bud.

By being here tonight, every one of you are helping to fight that stigma and helping a generation of children and young adults to becoming the generation that ends it.

My work and commitment for this charity, that I founded 14 years ago now, will never falter.

I and all those at Sentebale, be it here in London, Lesotho or Botswana -- will continue the work to make real long-lasting impact for all those that have been left vulnerable.

There's a lot to do, but it's only possible by working together and receiving support from people like yourselves... and like Lewis Capaldi... who has so generously flown here directly from Malaysia, via Dubai -- taking tonight out as a detour on his way to the Grammys in Los Angeles -- where he is nominated for best song.

Lewis, thank you for taking time out of your busy schedule to be with us this evening. We are all incredibly grateful."

Humanitarian activities

On April 7, 2020, Harry and Meghan unveiled the name of their future foundation "Archewell", from the ancient Greek word *archè,* meaning "source of action", which inspired their son's name Archie.

The Prince has learned to take advantage of the media attention he receives to publicize his charities (Sentebale Orphanage in Lesotho, Walking With The Wounded association for disabled war veterans, Kananelo Center for the Deaf near Maseru where he is learning the Dactylological Alphabet in Sign Language). This publicity allows him to attract donors. He initiated the Invictus Games, international multi-sport games for wounded and disabled soldiers.

Controversies and polemics

From adolescence, the prince is noticed for his antics. The media calls him "enfant terrible", the tabloid press calls him "Dirty Harry". At the age of 17, the tabloid press mentions his cannabis consumption, then altercations with paparazzi at the exit of nightclubs, excessive drinking (gin with a spoon...) and other blunders.

At the beginning of January 2005, he was photographed dressed as a Nazi at a masked ball, two weeks before the ceremonies commemorating the Jewish genocide in the United Kingdom. On January 11th, the tabloid *The Sun* published the photo on the front page under the title "Harry the Nazi", causing a scandal worldwide. A few days later, he apologized through a spokesperson.

In January 2009, the British tabloid *News of the World* unveiled a video in which the Prince calls "our little Paki friend" a soldier of Pakistani origin. His terms were described by David Cameron as "unacceptable" and by the *Daily Telegraph* as "racist".

In August 2012, he was photographed naked in a hotel suite in Las Vegas with several young women who were also naked.

In April 2017, Prince Harry explains his past escapades through a psychological trauma due to the death of his mother. He explains to the *Daily Telegraph* that it took him years to rebuild himself, with the help of therapists and his brother. He says, "I can say with confidence that losing my mother at the age of 12 and blocking all my emotions for the last twenty years has had a serious impact on my personal life, but also on my work.

Marriage and descent

Prince Harry was in a relationship from 2004 to 2011 with Chelsy Davy, daughter of a wealthy safari organizer, then with Cressida Bonas from 2012 to 2014.

On November 8, 2016, Kensington Palace officially announces his relationship with American actress Meghan Markle, three years his senior, whom he has been a companion since June 2016. One year later, on November

27, 2017, Prince Harry announced their engagement from the gardens of Kensington Palace.

The private ceremony was held in the Royal Chapel of St. James' Palace and was presided over by the Archbishop of Canterbury, Justin Welby. They were married shortly thereafter, on May 19, 2018, in St. George's Chapel at Windsor Castle and received the titles of Duke and Duchess of Sussex from the Queen on the same day.

On February 14, 2021, the couple announced that they were expecting a second child. On March 7, 2021, during the *Oprah* documentary *with Meghan and Harry*, the couple announced that they were expecting a little girl for the summer of 2021.

Titles and honours

Full title

As a grandson of the sovereign, he is prince of the United Kingdom of Great Britain and Northern Ireland with the predicate of Royal Highness. At birth, Prince Henry was named after his father's birthright, *Wales*. On the morning of his wedding day, May 19, 2018, Harry is titled by Queen Elizabeth II. His full title is from *His Royal Highness Prince Henry Charles Albert David, Duke of Sussex, Earl of Dumbarton, Baron Kilkeel*.

It is successively known under the following titles :

- September 15, 1984 - May 19, 2018 : *His Royal Highness* Prince Henry of Wales (*birth*) ;
- since May 19, 2018: *His Royal Highness* the Duke of Sussex.

As of March 31, 2020, he no longer uses his predicate of *Royal Highness, as* he is no longer active in the royal family.

Weapons

When Prince Harry came of age, as is customary in the British Royal Family, he was granted his own coat of arms by his grandmother Queen Elizabeth II. Traditionally, this is the coat of arms of the United Kingdom, broken by a five-point label with an element from his mother's coat of arms (the scallops found on the Spencer coat of arms). His brother, Prince William, has the same type of coat of arms but with a three-point break.

Part 2: Meghan Markle, Duchess of Sussex

Meghan Markle, born on August 4, 1981 in Los Angeles, is an American actress who became a member of the British royal family.

She became known as an actress through her role as Rachel Zane in the court TV series *Suits: Custom Lawyers*.

On May 19, 2018, she married Prince Harry, the youngest son of Prince Charles and Diana, grandson of Queen Elizabeth II, and became Duchess of Sussex.

After putting her career on hold during her engagement in November 2017, she and her husband decided in the spring of 2020 to distance themselves from the royal family and lead a financially independent life.

Biography

Childhood and education

Rachel Meghan Markle was raised in Los Angeles. Her parents are American, her mother, Doria Loyce Ragland (born September 15, 1956), is African-American and her father, Thomas Wayne Markle (born 1944), is of German, English, and Irish descent. Her mother is a yoga teacher and her father was a director of photography for television and film for forty years. Meghan Markle spent part of her childhood with her father, very often on the sets of *Married... with Children*.

She has a half-sister Samantha Markle, born in 1965 and a half-brother Thomas Markle Jr. born in 1967 from her father's first marriage.

She studied in private schools in Los Angeles, and was then admitted to Northwestern University in Chicago, Illinois, where she obtained a double bachelor's degree in theater and international relations in 2003. As part of her internship, she worked at the U.S. Embassy in Buenos Aires, Argentina. After having failed in the competitions that could open the door to a career in politics, she chose to devote herself entirely to film after her studies. The following year, she met producer Trevor Engelson, whom she married after seven years together.

Her *curriculum vitae*, published on Mail Online, mentions that she speaks Spanish fluently and is proficient in French.

Career

2000's: modeling and discreet beginnings

Meghan Markle made her first screen appearance in 2002 in the soap opera *Hospital Central* as a simple extra. At the beginning of her career, she confesses that she had difficulties finding major roles: "I wasn't black enough for black roles and I wasn't white enough for white, which left me somewhere in the middle as the ethnic chameleon who couldn't find a job". To pay her bills, she turned to freelance and part-time calligraphy, including personalized calligraphy on wedding invitation cards.

Meghan Markle then made her debut on the U.S. television show *Deal or No Deal on* April 12, 2006. She is the model wearing briefcase number 24, except for one appearance where she is wearing briefcase number 11. In early 2007, she left this program. On the occasion of the announcement of her engagement to Prince Harry, the media were quick to report on her participation in the program. A young woman with a plunging neckline and a scarlet satin miniskirt was shown in poses that the media deemed inappropriate for a future member of a royal family.

She played a minor role in the romantic comedy *7 Years of Seduction* (*A Lot Like Love*), released in 2005, and carried by the actor duo Ashton Kutcher and Amanda Peet, or in the TV movies *L'Amour hors limites* (*Deceit*) in 2006 and *The Apostles* by David McNally in 2009.

Moreover, according to her, making only appearances or playing only minor roles for about ten years (from 2000 to 2010), has never discouraged her.

Years 2010: television and media revelation

In 2010, his partner Trevor Engelson produced the feature film *Remember Me* and won him a role alongside Robert Pattinson and Emilie de Ravin. This film, with a budget of 16 million dollars, revealed her to the general public and allowed her to play in the comedy *American Trip* (*Get Him to the Greek*) with Jonah Hill and then in an episode of *CSI: Miami*, the most famous crime series of the moment.

In 2011, she finally landed a major role in the television series *Suits: Customized Lawyers and* will play in it for the first seven seasons. In this courtroom comedy, broadcast on USA Network, she plays Rachel Zane, a talented paralegal. The same year, she made an appearance in the hit comedy *How to Kill Your Boss*. The following year, she appeared on the set of the very popular detective series *Castle* for one episode and played in the independent dramatic comedy drama *Dysfunctional Friends* with Stacey Dash and Meagan Good.

This was followed by the comedy *Random Encounters* (2013), which she co-wrote with Michael Rady, then the romantic TV movie *The Spark of Love* (2014), directed by Gary Yates and starring Canadian actor Lochlyn Munro, and the *Anti-Social* thriller directed by British director Reg Traviss, nominated for Best Picture Fantasporto. In 2016, she is at the heart of a love triangle in the romantic comedy

How to Meet Your Soulmate in 10 Lessons with Kristoffer Polaha and Jonathan Scarfe.

In 2016, she was chosen to become *brand ambassador* (advertising muse) for the Canadian department store chain Reitmans.

In 2017, following her engagement to Prince Harry, she announced her departure from the series *Suits* at the end of the seventh season and decided to interrupt her acting career. Because of this royal commitment, she also decides to close her Instagram account, which counts 1.9 million *followers*, as well as the website she has been hosting since May 2014, *The Tig,* a lifestyle advice site (food, travel, fashion and beauty).

Between her acting fees, her lifestyle blogging revenues and her advertising contracts, her personal fortune in 2018 is estimated at approximately $5 million.

The 2020s

In the spring of 2020, she withdrew from the royal family and moved with her husband and son to the Los Angeles area and plans to resume her career in Hollywood.

Racist attacks

On January 14, 2018, the British press unveiled the text messages of Jo Marney, the girlfriend of Henry Bolton, leader of the political party UKIP. In these exchanges, the twenty-five year old woman makes violent comments about Meghan Markle. According to her, the genes of Prince Harry's fiancée "will defile our royal family" and lead straight to a "Muslim Prime Minister" and then a "black king". "It's the UK, not Africa," she said. She added that Meghan Markle would be "a silly little commoner, a stupid actress no one has ever heard of. Following the publication of these remarks, Henry Bolton disagreed with his girlfriend's speech and announced that he had decided to separate from her. Jo Marney eventually apologized, explaining that her messages were not intended to be made public.

Humanitarian commitment

Meghan Markle was chosen in 2014 and 2016 to speak at the annual One Young World (known as the "Davos Youth Forum") summits in Dublin and Ottawa respectively on the themes of gender equality and modern slavery. In December 2014, she travels to Spain and then to Afghanistan as part of the *United Service Organizations'* morale tour, chaired by the Chief of Staff of the U.S. Army, to support the morale of the troops. She also collaborates in 2015 with the United Nations Entity for Gender Equality and the Empowerment of Women (or UN Women), as a media spokesperson, at the Beijing summit where she gives a notable speech,. In 2016, she became a global ambassador for the NGO World Vision, traveling to Rwanda for the "*Clean Water*" campaign to provide safe and clean drinking water and to India to raise awareness on women's rights issues.

Meghan Markle defines herself as a feminist. In 2018, *Time* magazine named her one of the "100 Most Influential People in the World".

Privacy Policy

American businesswoman Bonnie Hammer (en) is one of the most important mentors in her career.

On August 16, 2011, she married in Jamaica, after seven years of living together, the Californian producer Trevor Engelson, whom she divorced in August 2013

In May 2016, she broke up with Canadian chef Cory Vitiello after a two-year relationship.

Royal Wedding

On November 8, 2016, her relationship with Prince Harry was officially announced and she has been his companion since June 2016. One year later, on November 27, 2017, Prince Harry announced their engagement from the gardens of Kensington Palace.

It is of Protestant denomination until March 6, 2018, the day on which it is baptized and confirmed in the Anglican religion. The private ceremony was celebrated in the Royal Chapel of St. James' Palace and was presided over by the Archbishop of Canterbury, Justin Welby. They were married shortly thereafter, on May 19, 2018, in St. George's Chapel at Windsor Castle and received the titles of Duke and Duchess of Sussex from the Queen on the same day She is the second divorced American to join the royal family after Wallis Simpson.

From the beginning of his relationship with Prince Harry, his look and fashion accessories are copied, this phenomenon being called by the press *"Meghan sparkle"* or "Meghan effect".

Meghan Markle makes her first official appearance as Duchess of Sussex and member of the Royal Family three days after her marriage at Prince Charles' garden party, celebrating her charity work and her 70th birthday, six months early.

On October 15, 2018, Kensington Palace announces that the couple is expecting their first child in the spring of 2019. Their son Archie Mountbatten-Windsor was born on May 6, 2019, becoming seventh in the order of succession to the British throne.

In July 2020, she miscarried while caring for her son Archie.

On February 14, 2021, the couple announced that they were expecting a second child. On March 7, 2021, during the *Oprah* documentary *with Meghan and Harry*, the couple announced that the child they were expecting for the summer of 2021 was a girl.

Departure of the royal family

After putting her career on hold during her engagement in November 2017, she and her husband decided in the spring of 2020 to distance themselves from the royal family, lead a financially independent life and settle in North America. She retains her title of Duchess of Sussex but will no longer use her predicate of Royal Highness.

She could have become a British citizen as a result of her marriage, but this process can take several years and should not be completed as she is no longer a resident of the United Kingdom.

Titles

Title

By birth a commoner, Meghan Markle has no title of nobility. She bears by marriage the title of her husband and her official title is "Her Royal Highness the Duchess of Sussex, Countess of Dumbarton, Baroness Kilkeel".

The common name "Princess Meghan" is incorrect because it is reserved for princesses of blood. Being a princess only by marriage, she is *Princess Henry* (as wife of Prince Henry). Only a decree of the Queen (as was the case for Prince Philip or Princess Alice) would allow the Duchess of Sussex to bear the title "Princess Meghan".

It bears successively the name then title of :

- August 4, 1981 - May 18, 2018: *Ms Rachel Meghan Markle* ;

- since May 19, 2018: *Her Royal Highness the Duchess of Sussex*".

As of March 31, 2020, she no longer uses her predicate of Royal Highness, as she is no longer active in the royal family.

Coat of Arms

Traditionally, wives of members of the British Royal Family combine their father's coat of arms with those of their new husband to create their own. However, in recent years, in the absence of a paternal coat of arms, designs by the College of Arms had been necessary for the fathers of Sophie Rhys-Jones and Catherine Middleton when they joined the Royal Family.

Contrary to this recent tradition, Thomas Markle (who is American) will not be granted a coat of arms, by decision of Queen Elizabeth II. Instead, the College of Arms indicated that Meghan Markle would be granted her own coat of arms directly. This was already the case in 1972 when Richard of Gloucester married Birgitte van Deurs (who was born Danish).

The weapons are unveiled on May 25, 2018 and are the result of a collaboration between the College of Arms and Meghan Markle to make them both "personal and representative". The azure background on the right side represents the Pacific Ocean off the coast of California; two gold shells symbolize the sun shining on the Duchess's home state; three feathers represent communication and the power of words. The terrace on which the arms are placed is composed of California poppy flowers, and Chimonanthus praecox which grows in Kensington Palace. The shield is supported by a lion crowned in English gold and a silver sparrow.

Ancestry

On her mother's side, Meghan Markle is descended, among others, from a great-great-great-grandfather who was a slave on Georgia's cotton plantations until 1865, when he was freed when slavery was abolished.

On her father's side, Meghan Markle counts among her distant ancestors King Edward III of England, whose Prince Harry is also a descendant in many branches.

Part 3: Marriage of Prince Harry and Meghan Markle

The **marriage of Prince Henry, Duke of Sussex and Meghan Markle** took place on May 19, 2018 at St. George's Chapel in Windsor, United Kingdom.

Couple

Prince Harry, made "Duke of Sussex" on his wedding day, is the youngest son of Charles, Prince of Wales and Lady Diana Spencer, and the grandson of Queen Elizabeth II and Prince Philip, Duke of Edinburgh.

Meghan Markle is an American actress known for her role as Rachel Zane in the court TV series *Suits: Custom Lawyers*. Divorced from producer Trevor Engelson, she is three years older than the prince.

Engagement Announcement

On November 8, 2016, it is officially announced that Meghan Markle is the companion of Prince Harry, with whom she has had a relationship since June 2016.

On November 27, 2017, the Prince announced his engagement to Meghan Markle. The next day, the wedding date is announced for May 19, 2018 in St. George's Chapel at Windsor Castle. Meghan could become British as a result of her marriage to Prince Harry. She will be the second divorced American woman to join the royal family after Wallis Simpson, for whom King Edward VIII had to abdicate in 1936.

Preparation and organization

On March 6, 2018, Meghan Markle was baptized and confirmed in the Anglican faith. The private ceremony was celebrated in the Royal Chapel of St. James' Palace and was presided over by the Archbishop of Canterbury, Justin Welby.

Ten children of honor (six girls and four boys) accompany the couple to the altar. Meghan Markle chose five: her two goddaughters Rylan and Remi Litt, and her best friend Jessica Mulroney's three children Brian, John and Ivy Mulroney. Harry chose Princess Charlotte and Prince George, as well as his three goddaughters Florence van Cutsem, Zalie Warren and Jasper Dyer.

Meghan Markle respects tradition with the bridal bouquet which, since the marriage of Princess Royal Victoria in 1858, has contained myrtle, an herb symbolizing love and hope. The bouquet also contains white forget-me-not flowers as a tribute to Princess Diana, whose favorite flowers they were, and flowers picked by Prince Harry himself the day before in the garden of their residence at Kensington Palace. As in previous royal weddings, the bouquet is sent after the wedding to Westminster Abbey to be laid on the Tomb of the Unknown Soldier, a tradition initiated by Elizabeth Bowes-Lyon at her wedding in 1923, in memory of her older brother Fergus, who died in 1915 at the Battle of Loos during the First World War. All other wedding flowers (St. George's Chapel floral decorations and compositions by London florist Philippa Craddock) will be donated to charity.

The couple respects tradition by not sleeping together the night before the wedding. Prince Harry spends the night with his brother and best man, Prince William, at the Coworth Park Hotel. Meghan Markle stays with her mother, Doria Ragland, at Cliveden House.

Meghan Markle, not being able to choose between her various relatives and not wanting to favour anyone, decided not to be accompanied by any witnesses.

Ducal title

A few hours before the ceremony, on the morning of May 19, 2018, Queen Elizabeth II bestowed upon Harry and Meghan the title of Duke and Duchess of Sussex.

Budget

The budget is not made public but the Bridebook site estimates it at a total of £32 million (€36.6 million). According to Kensington Palace, the royal family pays for the wedding mass, flowers, music and the reception that follows. Security is the main item in this budget (many drones and anti-UAV devices, security gantries, helicopters, various equipment and more than five thousand police officers, special forces, ambulance and firemen deployed). Estimated at £30 million, this security is entirely financed by the State.

According to estimates by the consulting firm Brand Finance (en), this marriage could bring more than a billion pounds (1.14 billion euros) to the United Kingdom, including 300 million to the tourism sector (spending, leisure, accommodation and transport), 300 million for "advertising made in Britain", 250 million for trade and catering, 50 million for derivatives.

Ceremony

The first of 2,640 people (1,200 youth, 200 members of charitable organizations, 100 students from nearby schools, 610 members of the castle community and 530 royal staff) invited into Windsor Castle Park to witness the arrival of the bride and groom and their guests, as well as the carriage procession, enter the park at 10:30 a.m. Nearly 100,000 people come to cheer Meghan Markle and Prince Harry in the City of Windsor. According to the *Daily Express*, the wedding is watched by an estimated 1.9 billion viewers.

The celebration, led by Windsor Dean David Conner (en), begins at 12:00 p.m. The couple marries in the traditional rite of the Anglican Church of England.

Prince Harry and his witness, his brother Prince William, arrive on foot from the west steps of the chapel. They are dressed in a Blues and Royals military frock coat made of midnight-blue deerskin with various decorations and barathea (en) pants with a red leather band. Meghan Markle arrives in a Rolls-Royce Phantom VI and enters the chapel through the Galilee Porch. She presents herself with a Givenchy wedding dress designed by Clare Waight Keller, wearing a low bun topped with a diamond tiara offered by the queen, dating from 1932 on a brooch from 1893. In the absence of her sick father, held back by heart surgery in Mexico, she walks up the central aisle of St. George's Chapel alone, before being joined halfway up the aisle by her father-in-law, Prince Charles.

During the procession of *Introït*, David Blackadder, trumpet player from the Orchestra of the *Age of Enlightenment* and the Academy of Ancient Music, dialogues with the Welsh soprano Elin Manahan Thomas (en) in an aria with orchestra, taken from a secular cantata by Georg Friedrich Haendel (organist, harpsichordist and court composer in the 18th century). It is more precisely an adaptation by the performers of the aria *Eternal Source of Light Divine* taken from the cantata composed in 1713 by Handel on the *Ode* for the Birthday of Queen Anne.

Lady Jane Fellowes, sister of Diana Spencer, reads an excerpt from King Solomon's *Song of Songs, an* earthly love poem from the Bible (8:6: "Put me as a seal upon your heart"). The poem as a whole relates the loves of the King of Israel and the Queen of Sheba, an African and Yemeni sovereign. Justin Welby, Archbishop of Canterbury, officiates for the exchange of consents. After pronouncing their vows, Prince Harry and Meghan Markle exchange wedding rings made by the British jewelry house Cleave and Company. Harry's ring is made of textured platinum and the bride's ring contains a few carats of Welsh gold nugget offered by Queen Elizabeth II (a royal tradition dating back to the marriage of Queen Mother Elizabeth in 1923, who was presented with a wedding ring from the Clogau Gold Mine by King George VI). The colorful keynote address is given by the American Pastor Michael Bruce Curry, Presiding Bishop of the Episcopal Church of the United States, who is noted for his passionate sermon.

The choir of St. George's Chapel in Windsor is directed by its choirmaster, James Vivian. It is composed of 23 soprano-boys (the *boy choristers*) and 12 professional adult choristers (the *Lay Clerks*), all men, according to the tradition dating back to 1348 for this choir (men providing the lower parts, from alto to bass). They performed *a cappella* a text from the Gospel according to St. John (John 14: 15-17), specific to the Christian feast of Pentecost and set to music in the form of a polyphonic *Anthem* (*If Ye Love Me*) by Thomas Tallis, a 16th century English composer. They performed another vocal piece, the motet *The Lord bless you and keep you* by contemporary English composer John Rutter. For some pieces requiring instruments, they were accompanied by a chamber orchestra, including a flute and harp, which brought together members of the BBC National Orchestra of *Wales*, the English Chamber Orchestra and the Philharmonia Orchestra (with the musicians largely coming from the string section of each orchestra). The conductor is Christopher Warren-Green.

Trumpets from the Royal Cavalry were used at several points during the ceremony: for the anthem Lord of *all hopefulness, Lord of all joy (*by Jan Struther, to traditional Irish music, *Slane*), for the Welsh anthem *Cwm Rhondda* and for the *God Save the Queen*. The organ is held by Luke Bond, assistant to James Vivian, the music master of St. George's Chapel.

The famous English gospel choir The Kingdom Choir ("The Kingdom Choir"), based in south-east London and conducted by Karen Gibson, performed (in connection with the gospel of the day) a choral arrangement of the soul standard: *Stand by me, by* Ben E. King, with keyboard accompaniment. Their performance was very well received. They closed the ceremony with a traditional gospel: *Amen (en)/This little light of mine (en)*.

This closing *Amen* followed a purely secular orchestral episode intended to initiate the exit procession: the *Allegro from* the Symphony No. 1 in B flat major by William Boyce, an 18th-century English composer. The young cellist Sheku Kanneh-Mason (en), aged 19, who had been spotted by Prince Harry, had played a transcription for cello and orchestra of : *Après* un *Rêve*, a melody originally written for voice and piano by the French composer Gabriel Fauré. The original text, sung, is not religious (but it did not exist here). He also played, again in an adaptation, a Sicilian (also secular form) supposed to date from the 18th century (but in reality apocryphal). It is the best known work of a composer who is not the author. We then heard, still with the orchestra, the (very) famous *Ave Maria* by Franz Schubert. This score and that of Gabriel Fauré, which remain very widespread, had been given, in different transcriptions, at the funeral of Johnny Hallyday at the Madeleine church in Paris.

The 600 guests at the religious service received a 22-page guide listing the rules of decorum to be respected. This guide notably forbids any electronic device (camera, photo camera, smartphone) likely to take photos or videos of the ceremony. The dress code imposes a suit or tails for men, a cocktail dress and a hat for women.

After signing the registers, the couple exchange a kiss on the stoop in front of the crowd. Following the religious ceremony at 1:00 p.m., accompanied by an escort from the Royal Household Mounted Cavalry Regiment, the couple took a carriage ride through the streets of Windsor (Castle Hill, High Street, downtown Windsor). Harry and Meghan have chosen an Ascot carriage, one of five of the Royal Mews, stables of the British Royal Family. The procession in an open carriage drawn by four Windsor Grey horses, takes them via the elm-lined Long Walk back to Windsor Castle Park where the 2,640 people are invited with prayer to bring their personal picnic, while the couple and the 600 guests at the church service are invited at 1:30 p.m. to a lunch hosted by Queen Elizabeth II in the Castle's Festival Hall. The cocktail menu includes Scottish langoustines, English asparagus, a pea panna cotta with quail eggs and lemongrass. During this meal, Elton John takes to the piano to sing several songs: *Tiny Dancer*, *I'm Still Standing,* and *Your Song*, a melody about love performed in homage to Princess Diana. Then the couple and the royal family pose for the official photos taken by photographer Alexi Lubomirski.

Throughout the ceremony, lip-reading specialists from the kingdom tried to decipher the words spoken by Prince Harry and Meghan Markle.

The father of the groom is hosting a private party for the family and 200 of his closest guests at 7:30 p.m. on the grounds of Frogmore House. The couple in evening dress (black velvet tuxedo for Prince Harry, white dress with American neckline and bare back signed Stella McCartney for Meghan Markle) arrive at the party in a vintage blue-silver Jaguar Type E, converted to an electric model, with a license plate bearing "E190518" (May 19, 2018, the date of their wedding). The dinner is closed with a set piece that shakes up British royal traditions, breaking with the classic candied fruit pudding. This royal cake, made with organic ingredients, is created by Claire Ptak and costs 57,000 euros. It is an organic lemon sponge cake from the Amalfi coast with elderflower covered with buttercream and fresh flowers. The opening of the ball is Whitney Houston's *I Wanna Dance with Somebody.* During the evening, guests danced to songs from the 1980s and R&B, with DJ Idris Elba.

Enjoy all our books for free...

  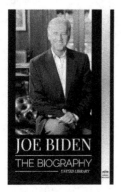

Interesting biographies, engaging introductions, and more.

Join the exclusive United Library reviewers club!

You will get a new book delivered in your inbox every Friday.

Join us today, go to: https://campsite.bio/unitedlibrary

BOOKS BY UNITED LIBRARY

Kamala Harris: The biography

Barack Obama: The biography

Joe Biden: The biography

Adolf Hitler: The biography

Albert Einstein: The biography

Aristotle: The biography

Donald Trump: The biography

Marcus Aurelius: The biography

Napoleon Bonaparte: The biography

Nikola Tesla: The biography

Pope Benedict: The biography

Pope Francis: The biography

Bitcoin: An introduction to the world's leading cryptocurrency

And more...

See all our published books here:
https://campsite.bio/unitedlibrary

ABOUT UNITED LIBRARY

United Library is a small group of enthusiastic writers. Our goal is always to publish books that make a difference, and we are most concerned with whether a book will still be alive in the future. United Library is an independent company, founded in 2010, and now publishing around up to 50 books a year.

Joseph Bryan - FOUNDER/MANAGING EDITOR

Amy Patel - ARCHIVIST AND PUBLISHING ASSISTANT

Mary Kim - OPERATIONS MANAGER

Mary Brown - EDITOR AND TRANSLATOR

Terry Owen - EDITOR

CPSIA information can be obtained
at www.ICGtesting.com
Printed in the USA
BVHW050540040821
613604BV00016B/387